Eric Begbie

Gundog Training
Made Easy

**An easy-to-follow guide to basic retriever and
spaniel training lessons complete with
Frequently Asked Questions**

Other books by Eric Begbie include:
Modern Wildfowling (1980 and 1989)
The Sportsman's Companion (1981)
The New Wildfowler – 3rd Edition (Ed.) (1987)
Fowler in the Wild (1988)
*Fowling in the Wild (2005)
*Gundog Training for the Duck and Goose Hunter (2006)
*A Waterfowler's Bedside Book (2006)

*also available from www.lulu.com

ISBN 1-4116-7029-9

Contents

The author with a young labrador puppy

Introduction

It is now over 25 years since the original version of Eric Begbie's Gundog Training Broadsheets was first published in Great Britain. From the very beginning, the Broadsheets revolutionised the training of retrievers and spaniels – not by making the process even more complicated than most of the books available at that time portrayed, but by simplifying the task into a series of logically structured and sequenced lessons.

These Broadsheets received considerable acclaim and have been used by thousands of amateur dog trainers in all five continents of the world. Crucially, they do not rely upon aversive training methods such as the use of electronic collars or forced pressure techniques involving pain or discomfort. The focus is on positive, reward-based training consistent with modern psychological principles. It is sometimes called the "British Method" but, of course, it works anywhere in the world wherever there are dog owners who want to train their hunting companions to the highest standards in a humane, pain-free manner.

The lessons contained within the Gundog Training Broadsheets were regularly updated to reflect modern practices and the advent of the Internet allowed a great deal of discussion of the methods to be enjoyed by hunters and dog trainers throughout the world. Inevitably many questions were raised and answered. Ultimately the most frequent of those questions were brought together and now form the second part of this book.

Follow this training course carefully and logically and you will be well on the road to having a well-trained gundog to join you on your hunting expeditions.

Lesson 1

TRAIN YOUR OWN GUNDOG

A well-trained dog is of immeasurable assistance to the shooting man or woman. The financial investment in a gundog is considerable when one considers that there is not only the outlay of £300 - £450 ($500 - $800) for a puppy from good working stock; the dog will cost upwards of £2500 ($4500) to feed and maintain during a normal canine lifetime. For this reason, if for no other, the owner should begin with a firm commitment to maximise the return on his investment by training his dog to an acceptable standard for service in the field. Working a well trained dog is immensely satisfying.

By concentrating the most important lessons in a series of easy-to-follow Lessons and by keeping production costs to the minimum, I have been able to provide this comprehensive gundog training course for not much more than the price of a good staghorn whistle and a couple of dummies! The amateur handler who follows the step-by-step instructions carefully and patiently should be able to train his gundog puppy to a reasonable level of competence within one year. Many users have said that these Lessons are far more helpful than more complicated books or videos.

Because the instructions contained within these Lessons are based firmly upon accepted scientific psychological principles they provide a very easy-to-follow system.

Individual owners may select those lessons which are appropriate to their intended use of their dog but it should be stressed that all the basic obedience and control exercises must be mastered before success with more specialised work can be expected. In this respect the Stop Whistle is probably the most important lesson of all.

Although initially designed for gundog breeds, the Lessons are also an ideal training aid for family pets and other working breeds. If your dog is intended only as a pet or companion, follow the lessons up to at least Lesson 6 plus the walking-to-heel exercise in Lesson 7. But why stop there? You and your dog can have a lot of fun together if you continue the course. Retrieving practice and water work are an ideal way of exercising a family pet.

A good gundog is a pleasure to work with and a positive asset in any hunting situation. It is, therefore, worth spending a good deal of time and energy on basic training. The Age Range and Duration given at the start of each Lesson are for guidance only. They provide a rough measure against which the trainer can assess the progress of his puppy but they should not be taken as definitive in every case. Some pups learn faster than others but even the "plodders" can make highly satisfactory gundogs if their owners have sufficient patience.

By using this training course you will be laying the foundations for a very rewarding relationship with your canine friend.

The first lesson is very simple. Make friends with your new puppy. Pups of all breeds love to play, so spend a few weeks enjoying being together. In the Supplementary Guidance later in this book, Topic 2 outlines some of the early training that can, without really trying, be accomplished during this period.

Lesson 2

Basic Approach; Training Aids
Approach

There are no mysteries about gundog training; neither are there any shortcuts. The path to success lies in a logical, ordered approach and in ensuring that the basic obedience and control exercises have been thoroughly mastered before progressing to more specialised work. Gundog training need not make onerous demands upon the handler's time but it is absolutely essential that regular sessions are set aside for the purpose. It is far better to have short daily periods of 15 - 20 minutes than to attempt to cram the lessons into an hour or two at weekends. Once the puppy becomes bored, he will not respond well to any attempt to continue a training session.

Before even contemplating buying a puppy, therefore, make a resolution to order your own life in such a way as to allow the necessary time for gundog training.

Secondly, read and re-read the next two Lessons which deal with canine psychology and underlying principles respectively. Far too many people profess to be gundog "experts" without even faintly knowing what makes a dog's brain tick. A thorough understanding of these topics is essential to a scientific approach to gundog training and you should feel comfortable with the concepts before proceeding.

Equipment

The following items of equipment will be useful as you progress with the training of your puppy. It would be wise to collect them together before training commences in order that each item will be to hand when required:

- 1 Slip Lead, preferably good quality rope
- 1 10 yard Check Cord
- 1 Gundog Whistle (e.g. Acme 211½)
- 1 Light Dummy (a sock stuffed with tissue will do)

- 3 Canvas Throwing Dummies (about 1 lb. weight each)
- 1 Dummy Launcher with three launcher dummies and a supply of blanks
- 1 Game Bag (for carrying equipment when training)

The dummy launcher is a fairly expensive item of equipment but it is worth having as it obviates the need for a starting pistol or shotgun adapter.

In America, dummies are sometimes known as "bumpers".

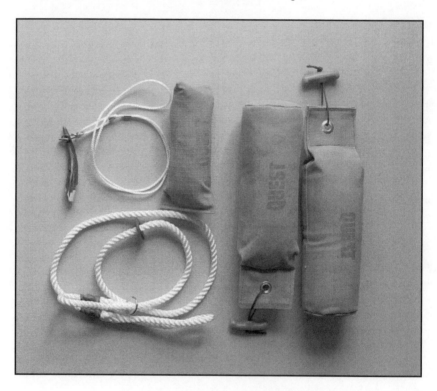

Some basic training equipment

Lesson 3

Response Reinforcement; Rewards and Punishment; Commands; Canine Psychology

Virtually all modern humane gundog training techniques are based upon a phenomenon which behavioural psychologists call operant conditioning. In essence this consists of reinforcing a desired response by providing a reward when it is correctly performed or eliminating an unwanted response by "punishment". The following sequence contains examples of stimuli, responses and reinforcing agents:

The handler blew a single blast on his whistle (stimulus) whereupon his labrador immediately stopped (response) "Good Boy" called the hander in a kindly voice. (reinforcement) He then called the dog's name (stimulus) and when it ran to him, (response) he gave it praise. (reinforcement)

Rewards and Punishment

The positive reinforcing agents used to reward correct responses should normally be petting or friendly praise. With a young puppy it is permissible to use edible rewards such as small biscuits or other treats for some of the initial training but these should be given simultaneously with verbal praise and be phased out as basic obedience training progresses. Punishment should not be required frequently but, when it is, a verbal scolding while holding the puppy by the loose skin under its neck is adequate. A dog should never be kicked or struck with a stick, whip or any other implement.

Verbal commands, whistle commands, hand signals and the sound of gunshot are all examples of stimuli to which appropriate responses are sought. The words which are used as commands should be short and phonetically distinct so as to avoid confusion.

Commands

The commands provide the stimuli to which the puppy will learn to respond. Verbal, whistle and hand signals will be used and, at a later stage, the sound of a shot or the flushing of game will also be stimuli to which responses are required. The following words are widely used as verbal commands:

Name	Used to summon dog's attention
Sit (or Hup)	Sit
Stay	Remain in sitting position (but see note below*)
Here	Come to Handler
Heel	Walk to heel
Hi-Seek	Quest for Game
Hi-Lost	Retrieve
Get-Over	Jump fence or ditch
No!	Stop doing that
Leave-it	Do not pick that up

If other words are used they should be short and not readily confused with each other. Stick absolutely rigidly to the words you decide to use. You cannot expect a dog to understand the word "Don't" if you normally use "No".

* Stay – A modern trend is to omit the "Stay" command and to simply use the command "Sit" to mean "Sit and stay sat until I tell you to move". This makes perfect sense and it is really a matter of personal preference whether or not you use a separate "Stay" command.

Lesson 4

Underlying Principles

The series of lessons which follows has been arranged in a time sequence which corresponds approximately to the age of the puppy. Dogs do vary quite considerably in the rate at which they learn so the age guide may have to be altered to suit an individual pupil. Throughout the lessons there are three very important principles which must be kept in mind at all times. An amateur trainer can easily slip up as a result of over-enthusiasm, tiredness, frustration, excitement or any number of other reasons but any deviation from these basic principles is a sure step towards failure.

Consistency - It is vital always to be consistent in the way a dog is treated. The same commands should always be used and the dog should never be asked to do something, e.g. chase an unshot hare, which would normally be forbidden. It is only too easy to fall into the trap of having one set of rules for some occasions and another set for different circumstances. Be particularly careful if you keep your dog in the house - your puppy cannot appreciate that it is acceptable for him to jump up at you or your wife but that he must not maul your mother-in-law or the postman.

Non-Predictability - Consistency should not be confused with predictability. A dog should never be able to predict its handler's commands so identical routines should not be followed every day. Different routes should be taken for exercise and training should be performed in varying sequences so that the dog has to await its owner's command rather than being able to predict the next move.

Insistence - Once the dog has been trained to give a certain response, correct performance must be insisted upon whenever the appropriate command is given. For example, if the dog has been commanded to "stay" and, after a few minutes, it wanders for a yard or two, then it must be taken back to the stay position and again commanded to stay. Even minor lapses of discipline will lead to an unreliable gundog if allowed to remain uncorrected.

Look for ways in which you can use everyday occurrences to reinforce the more formal training. As an example, once you have taught the puppy to sit and stay, make him sit while you put his food bowl down before him and then wait varying lengths of time before calling him forward to eat. Similarly, it might be possible for you to make him sit at the open kennel gate before taking him his evening walk. Wait until you have reached the garden gate before calling him up.

With little "extra" exercises of that sort, however, do be sure to avoid falling into the predictability-trap by varying the length of time you make him sit or the distance you walk away before calling him.

This is also the time when tone of voice will become established as both a rewarding and a punishing tool. Always use a kind tone of voice, along with physical petting, when you are praising your puppy for the correct performance of a response. Use a stern tone of voice when scolding him for an incorrect response.

The use of the word "No!" or "Bad Dog!" (your choice) in a stern voice will become the principle agent of punishment as you progress with the early training. Especially if you keep your puppy in your house, there will be many occasions in the early stages when you will have the opportunity to instill this disciplinary regime. Whenever the puppy does something that you do not want him to do, such as for example, chewing an electric cable or scratching a table leg or jumping up at a visitor, then *gently* grasp him by the loose skin under his neck and *gently* drag him from the "scene of the crime" while telling him "No!" in a stern tone of voice.

Lesson 5

Basic Obedience; Here - Sit - Stay

Normal Age Range: 3-5 months   Normal Duration: 4 weeks

OBJECT: To teach the puppy to come when called, to sit in response to a verbal command and to stay in one place when so instructed.

METHOD:

a) HERE - The "here" command is best taught in a confined space such as a garden lawn so that the pup cannot range too far away from you. Allow him to romp freely for a few minutes and then call his name in a firm but soft voice. If the pup starts towards you, give the command "here" repeatedly until he reaches you and then give a small biscuit and lots of praise as reinforcement. If the dog does not respond immediately, show him the biscuit and give the command "here" repeatedly as he approaches. Give him the biscuit and a kind word. Concentrate on the "here" command for at least a week and do not move on until the puppy comes to you every time the command is given. Gradually phase out the biscuit as part of the reward, giving praise and petting only.

(b) SIT - This response is probably the easiest of all to teach a dog. Place one hand under the pup's chin and the other on his rump. Give the command "sit" and, holding his chin up, press down on the puppy's rump so that the sitting position is adopted. Hold the pup there for a few seconds while you give reinforcement. Repeat this four or five times and then try giving the verbal command without touching the dog. If he sits, give praise and a biscuit. If not, show him again by holding his chin up and pressing down on the rump. Most pups will learn this in two or three days and then a week should be spent combining the "here" and "sit" commands by calling the dog to you and commanding him to sit when he arrives. Remember to give enthusiastic praise.

(c) STAY - Command the dog to sit and remain beside him for ten seconds. If, during this time, the dog starts to get up, repeat the sit command. After the pup has been sitting for ten seconds, say "stay" and slowly move back a few yards from him. If he starts to move, *gently* grip him by the loose skin beneath the neck, take him back to the exact spot from which he moved and again tell him to sit. Wait ten seconds, command him to stay and then slowly move away again. When the dog allows you to move three yards away, return to him and give praise and a biscuit as reinforcement. Each day increase the distance which you move away before returning to reinforce the response.

If you have decided to dispense with a separate "Stay" command and use "Sit" to mean "Sit and Stay", then simply repeat the "Sit" command in place of the "Stay" command in this exercise. After a few successful executions, begin to omit the repeated "Sit" command, relying on the first one to indicate "Sit and Stay".

PERFORMANCE: This exercise has been successfully taught when the dog comes to you every time it is called, sits immediately he is commanded and remains in one place when you walk away after telling him to stay. Increase the distance to about 100 yards and include occasions when you walk out of sight before calling him to you. All of these commands can be used whenever you have contact with the dog throughout the day, e.g. feeding times. You will appreciate that you must be able to rely upon the dog obeying those commands consistently before any further training should be attempted.

Lesson 6

Basic Obedience; Whistle and Hand Signals

Normal Age Range: 5-7 months   Normal Duration: 4 weeks

There will be times, both in future training and when you finally take your dog hunting, when it will be advantageous to be able to control the dog without using the voice. This lesson deals with substituting both whistle commands and hand signals for the verbal commands which the puppy has already learned. A good Staghorn or Acme Model 211½ dog whistle is recommended for beginners although some handlers prefer a "silent" whistle which has a very high pitch and, although audible to a dog, cannot be heard by the human ear.

OBJECT: To train the dog to sit and to come to the handler by using either whistle or hand signals and to train the dig to stop and sit at a distance from the handler by using the stop whistle.

METHOD:

(a) SIT - The puppy has already been trained to sit in response to a verbal stimulus. In order to elicit the same response to different stimuli, the accepted command and the new stimuli are provided simultaneously or in rapid succession. For the sit command these new stimuli are a single one second blast on the whistle and a hand signal consisting of raising the left hand above the head.

(i) Whistle - Call your dog to you, tell him to sit, follow the verbal command immediately with a single blast on the whistle and then give praise and petting as reinforcement. Command the pup to stay (if you are using the separate "Stay" command), walk ten yards away, call the pup to you and repeat the sitting routine with both verbal command and whistle. Repeat the whole exercise five times. On the sixth run-through, omit the verbal command, i.e. call the dog to you and, when he reaches your side, give the whistle command on its own. If the dog sits, give him lavish praise. If not, give the verbal command to sit, followed immediately by the whistle. Repeat this routine several times each day, gradually reducing the number of occasions on which the whistle is preceded by the verbal instruction. After a week you should find that the puppy will sit as readily to the whistle as he will to the verbal command.

(ii) Hand Signal - Once the dog is thoroughly familiar with the whistle command to sit, perform exactly the same routine but every time you make him sit, raise your left hand like a policeman stopping traffic. (If you normally carry your gun in your left hand, use the right hand for hand signals.) After a dozen examples of giving the hand signal simultaneously with either the verbal command or whistle, make the pup stay, walk a short distance away and then call him up. When he reaches you, give the hand signal without any other command. If the pup sits - which is fairly likely - praise him enthusiastically. If not, give the verbal command and repeat the exercise. Consolidate this training by using a mixture of all three modes of command whenever the pup is out of his kennel for training or exercise.

(b) HERE - The pup has already learned to come to you in response to the verbal command "here".

(i) Whistle - Command the dog to sit and stay. Walk on 25 - 30 yards. Stop, turn to face the pup, give the verbal command "here" and follow immediately with a series of three short toots on the whistle. The puppy might show some stickiness at this. If he does, repeat the verbal command and give lots of praise when he reaches you. Repeat several times until the dog shows no stickiness on hearing the whistle. After five or six runs through this routine, repeat the exercise without the verbal command. Continue until the whistle alone brings the pup to you every time that it is used.

(ii) Hand Signal - Repeat the above exercise but, at the same time as giving the whistle or verbal command, pat your left hand against your thigh several times. After five runs through this exercise make the dog sit and stay, walk on 25 - 30 yards and, without any verbal or whistle command, give the thigh pat signal. If he comes to you give lots of praise and petting to reinforce the response. If not, call him up verbally and repeat the exercise.

During this phase of the training you may very well find that you have been training yourself as well as your puppy. Do you now find that you automatically give the sit and come hand signals when giving verbal or whistle commands?

(c) THE STOP WHISTLE - Both in the hunting field and in future training there are many occasions when it is necessary to stop the dog wherever he is and hold him on the drop while awaiting further instructions. You have already trained him to sit in response to a single blast on the whistle while he is close to you. The stop command is simply an extension of this in that you must train the dog to stop and sit in response to the whistle wherever he is.

Allow the puppy to romp freely for a few minutes and, when he is about 10 yards away, give a single blast on the whistle. If he stops and sits, walk over to him and give plenty of praise and petting. If he does not stop and sit, take him back to the exact spot where he was when the whistle was blown, make him sit and adopt the following procedure:

Command him to sit, walk about 10 yards away and turn to face him. Command him to come and, when he is about half way, give the stop whistle and raise your left hand simultaneously. If he stops instantly, walk to him and give him praise. If not, take him back to the spot where he was when the stop command was given and make him sit. Repeat this process until he stops immediately the whistle and hand signal are given and then gradually phase out the hand signal. Continue with this exercise, gradually increasing the distance at which you give the stop whistle. In every case praise him if he does stop and correct him if he fails. The stop whistle is possibly the most important lesson in the whole training process and you should not move on to the next lesson until it is obeyed consistently.

At this stage you will have noticed one of the dilemmas that will re-occur throughout further training. You want to reward the dog but he is some distance away from you. In some cases you must walk to him to give praise, in some cases you might be able to tell him "Good Boy" in a loud enough voice to be audible. Don't allow the inconvenience of this deter you from praising him for correctly performed exercises. Later in the training schedule, after you have taught retrieving a dummy, you will be able to reward correct performance of basic exercises, at a distance, by giving a retrieve – an action that most gundogs certainly do find rewarding.

PERFORMANCE: Once this section of your gundog training is completed, the puppy should come to you whenever called by voice, whistle or hand signal and should stop and sit whenever commanded by verbal, whistle or hand signal.

The stop whistle is probably the most important lesson in the whole course and you should not attempt to move on until it is obeyed perfectly every time.

Lesson 7

Gunshot; Walking to Heel

Normal Age Range: 6-7 months   Normal Duration: 2 weeks

GUNSHOT

OBJECT: To ensure that the puppy becomes accustomed to the sound of gunshot and, in the case of spaniels or roughshooter's retrievers, to train the dog to drop to shot.

METHOD: Accustom the dog to the sound of shot by asking a friend to take a starting pistol or dummy launcher 100 yards away. Command the pup to sit beside you and signal your friend to fire a shot. If the pup merely looks towards the sound and shows no fear or alarm, give him praise. If he is startled a little, soothe and reassure him. Over a period of days, repeat the exercise, each time bringing the sound of the shot a little nearer the pup until he shows no alarm when it is very close to him. Unless you are training a retriever specifically for field trials, it is advantageous to train a dog to drop to shot. This is a great help to maintaining steadiness and is achieved by repeating the stop whistle exercise from Lesson 6 but substituting the sound of a shot for the single blast on the whistle. After the pup is accustomed to the sound of a starting pistol or dummy launcher, the exercise should be repeated using a shotgun fired into the air. This training can continue for a few weeks and may overlap the next lesson without harm.

WALKING TO HEEL

OBJECT: To train the dog to walk in pace with its handler, level with his knee.

METHOD: It is essential that a gundog is trained to walk in pace with his handler. Walking to heel need not be taught in special training sessions. Indeed, it is probably more convenient to deal with it when simply walking the dog for exercise. A rope slip lead is most suitable and, contrary to popular belief, it will not harm your pup. A gundog should always walk to heel at the left side of the handler, unless he happens to be a left-handed Shot.

With the dog on a short lead, walk with him at your left side. Every 10 seconds or so, tighten the lead enough to check the dog and give the verbal command "heel". After a day or two allow some slack in the lead. If the dog moves ahead, pull him back sharply as you give the "heel" command. Once he will walk on a slack lead without pulling, it is time to remove the lead. Carry your whistle at this stage and if the dog leaves the heel position, give the command "heel". Should he respond, give him praise. If not, blow the stop whistle, walk up to him, wait for 30 seconds and then put his lead on and start again. The pause is very important as the dog must not think that he is being punished for obeying the stop whistle. It will assist this lesson if, for the first few weeks, the dog is walked at heel situated between the handler and a wall or fence. It is doubtful if the pup can differentiate between the commands "here" and "heel" and he will probably come to regard either as an instruction to come to the handler and walk to heel.

PERFORMANCE: At the end of this stage the dog should walk to heel without a lead and, if a shot is fired, he should show no fear. A spaniel or roughshooter's dog should sit when a shot is fired; formal retrievers should continue to walk at heel, ignoring the shot. By the way, if you are an American, then you may be more familiar with the terms "Upland Game Hunting" and "Waterfowling" rather than the equivalent British terms "Roughshooting" and "Wildfowling".

Lesson 8

Retrieving a Dummy

Normal Age Range: 6-9 months   Normal Duration: 4 weeks

OBJECT: To train the puppy to retrieve an artificial dummy to hand when commanded.

METHOD: The best way to start a puppy retrieving is to play games with the dummy until he is quite happy about running to it and picking it up in his mouth. Use a light dummy at this stage and carry out these first games in a confined passageway so that the pup cannot run away with the dummy. This is a time when you must be very gentle with the pup.

Do not attempt to snatch or pull the dummy from him or allow "tug o' war" situations to develop. If he is reluctant to come to you with the dummy, try walking backwards away from him, calling him gently as you do so. Do not allow him to carry a dummy, or any other object, around outwith training sessions as there is a danger that he will come to regard the dummy as "his" rather than "yours". Once he appears to have got the hang of picking a dummy up and bringing it to you, proceed with the more formal retriever training as follows:

- Call the dog to you and command him to sit.
- Hold him gently but firmly and throw the dummy a distance of about six yards. Do not allow the puppy to move.
- Release your hold on him, giving the stay command as you do so.
- After 20 seconds give the retrieve command "hi-lost" (or "fetch" if you prefer) and signal with your arm in the direction of the dummy.
- If the dog goes out and picks up the dummy, call him to you immediately with both the verbal command and hand signal (pat thigh).
- As soon as he arrives back, give lots of praise and take the dummy from him very gently.

That may all sound very simple but there are several different things which can go wrong with that single exercise. Treat any problems as follows:

- If the dog succeeds in getting away from you when you throw the dummy or fails to stay when you release him, use the stop whistle immediately to stop him before he reaches the dummy. If he fails to stop, ignore the dummy training for five minutes and give some "come-sit-stay-come-stop" exercises. Then try again with the dummy.
- If he does not go out for the dummy when you give the retrieve command and hand signal (bear in mind that he has not yet been taught either), go to the dummy yourself, call up the dog and try again by throwing the dummy a shorter distance and keeping the dog at the stay position for only five seconds.
- If the pup picks up the dummy but does not bring it to you when called, use the stop whistle, make him sit (still holding the dummy) and walk backwards away from him. At about 12 paces call him to you and give the "here" hand signal. When he does come to you, give a lot of praise before, during and after taking the dummy from him.

Good stylish retrieving is a very desirable quality in both retrievers and spaniels and it will pay to spend a whole month working at this basic level. Gradually increase the distance you throw the dummy, increase the weight of the dummy and increase the length of time you hold the puppy on the drop before sending him to retrieve. Towards the end of the month you may start to use a dummy launcher for some of the retrieves but do not overdo it at this stage and only use the launcher at half power, i.e. with the dummy pushed halfway down the spindle.

PERFORMANCE: By the end of this lesson your gundog puppy should be able to retrieve a visually marked dummy on command and will be steady to a thrown dummy, i.e. he will not run-in before he is told to do so.

CONSOLIDATION: At this point in the dog's training, each session should last about 20 minutes and variety should be added to the exercises by mixing retrieving practice with some "come-sit-stay" work, utilising verbal, whistle and hand signals.

Keep the basic principles from Lesson 4 firmly in mind at all times. There will be bad days - either because you or the pup is not in the mood (probably more often you!!). On such days try hard to take things easy. No matter how difficult a training session has been, always end it with an exercise which you know the puppy can perform well in order that you can finish with a lot of praise before you put him back in his kennel

You will have noted how important it was to have the basic obedience and stop whistle completed before starting the retrieving exercises.

However, having said that, if your puppy was from good working lines of one of the established retriever breeds such as a labrador, you may well have discovered that his natural retrieving instincts made this lesson "as easy as pie". Although I have left this basic retrieving training until after basic obedience has been instilled, many owners will have been tempted to play "fetch" games at an earlier stage. There is no harm in this just as long as you remain in charge and the games do not lead to bad habits or indiscipline.

There is always a lot of discussion amongst trainers, especially in America, about whether separate commands such as "Hold" and "Give" should form part of retrieving training. They often form part of what is euphemistically described as a "force fetch" regime. In my experience, a puppy from good working stock should possess natural retrieving instincts and should not require this type of training.

WARNING: Under no circumstances be tempted to take the dog out shooting or hunting at this stage. You are still a long way from the day when your puppy will be ready to accompany you on a shoot. More gundogs have been spoiled from two causes than from all the other reasons put together. The two causes are:

- Lack of basic obedience training
- Premature introduction to the shooting field.

DO NOT BE HASTY!

Lesson 9

Directional Control

Normal Age Range: 8-10 months Normal Duration: 5 weeks

OBJECT: To train the dog to go out to either side or away from the handler in response to directional hand signals.

METHOD: Armed with two dummies, sit the dog facing you with about five yards between you and him. Command him to stay. Throw one dummy about 10 yards to your left, wait 10 seconds and throw the other dummy 10 yards to your right.

Wait another 10 seconds and then, signalling boldly with your left arm, give the retrieve command. If the dog moves in the correct direction, allow him to retrieve the dummy and give a lot of praise. If, on the other hand, he starts off in the wrong direction, stop him immediately with the stop whistle, lead him halfway to the correct dummy and send him to retrieve it from there. The essence of this exercise is to reward with praise when he moves in the correct direction but to stop him immediately and re-command if he starts off in the wrong direction.

After he has retrieved the left-hand dummy, make him sit for 10 seconds and then send him for the right-hand dummy, using the retrieve command and a bold signal with the right arm. Once more praise him if he gets it right or stop him immediately if he heads the wrong way. Repeat this exercise over a period of seven days, varying the order in which you send the pup in each direction. Occasionally send him for one dummy, make him sit, throw it again and make him retrieve it a second time before sending him for the other dummy.

When he can retrieve two dummies from either side to command, repeat the procedure but throw a third dummy straight out behind the dog in addition to those to the right and left. Use an overhead "push" wave of the arm when sending him straight out for the dummy behind. After a further two weeks of practice at this exercise with hand-thrown dummies, use the dummy launcher at half power to give longer retrieves in each direction and occasionally give an extra-long retrieve with the launcher at full power.

Once the dog responds correctly to directional hand signals when retrieving visually marked dummies, you can move on to directing him to a hidden dummy using the same hand signals and commands. Place a dummy out of the dog's sight and walk with him to within 20 yards of it. Send him straight out towards it with an overhead wave and the verbal retrieve command. If he deviates markedly from the correct path, stop him with the whistle and correct his course with the appropriate directional hand signal. By varying the position of the dummy and the initial direction in which you send the dog, you can give practice at responding to all three directional signals when he is working out in front of you. Remember that it is essential to stop him immediately he starts to move in any direction other than the one which you have indicated.

PERFORMANCE: At the conclusion of this stage you should be able to command your dog to move in any direction using hand signals.

At this stage in your dog's training it is vital to introduce another two principles. The first is that not every dummy is his to retrieve. You must get him used to this concept so that he does not continue to anticipate that every thrown dummy is automatically followed by a retrieve command. From now on, whenever you are practising retrieving, make a point of walking over and picking up every second or third dummy yourself.

The second principle is what the behaviourists call "intermittent re-inforcement". Experiments have shown that behaviour patterns are re-inforced more solidly if only a proportion of correct responses are rewarded. So, from now on, make a point of rewarding only every second or third correct performance of any command.

Lesson 10

Following a Scent; Questing Ahead

Normal Age Range: 9-11 months Normal Duration: 4 weeks

FOLLOWING A SCENT

So far we have relied upon visual marking of the dummy but one of the main attributes of a good gundog is the ability to use its nose to find dead or wounded game. We want to train the dog to follow a ground scent such as would be left by a wounded bird.

Leaving the puppy in the car or held by a friend, make a scent trail by tying a dummy to a long piece of string, attaching it to a long pole and then, keeping the dummy at pole's length from yourself, drag it along the ground for about 20 yards and leave it out of sight of the starting point. Still keeping yourself as far from the dummy as possible, cut the string. Take a route back which does not cross the trail.

Now bring the dog to the start point of the trail and, without any hand signals, give the verbal command to retrieve (Hi-lost). Should he go in the wrong direction entirely, use the stop whistle, bring him back and start again. Some dogs learn to follow a scent much more quickly than others and, in sticky cases, it might be necessary to direct the pup along the trail by hand before he gets the hang of using his nose. Repeat the exercise each day, gradually laying longer and more twisted trails and trails through patches of rough cover.

QUESTING AHEAD

All spaniels and also other breeds used by roughshooters should be trained to quest ahead of the handler to spring game within shot of the Guns. Many dogs are natural questers and those which might have been a bit sticky should have been loosened-up by the scenting exercise and by retrieving blind retrieves.

Start training on ground where there is unlikely to be much game and aim to keep the dog moving within a rectangle ten yards in front and ten yards to either side of you. Later you will extend the range a little but it is better to start with a restricted questing limit. Using the command "Hi-seek", wave the dog out in front of you. When he reaches the ten yard limit give two short peeps on the whistle and, having thus attracted his attention, signal him out to the right, again giving the command "Hi-seek". When he reaches ten yards to your right, once more give two short peeps and signal him to the left with the same verbal command and hand signal. When he reaches ten yards to the left, stop him with the whistle, walk up to him and give him praise.

After three days of this exercise, start slowly walking forward as you work him from side to side in front of you. Always use the whistle when he reaches the limit in any direction and give bold arm signals and the command "Hi-seek" at every change of direction. Praise often but intermittently.

Should a bird or rabbit be flushed during this exercise, stop the dog immediately with the stop whistle. Move to ground which will hold game and encourage him to investigate bushes or clumps of rough as he quests from side to side. Be ready to stop him if anything flushes.

Use bold arm signals

Lesson 11

Entering and Crossing Water; Jumping Obstacles

Normal Age Range: 10-12 months
Normal Duration: 1-2 weeks

WATER WORK

Many gundog puppies will have entered water spontaneously by the time they are a few months old but, if yours has not had the opportunity to do so or has shown some reluctance, now is the time to get him into the swim. For a first encounter with water choose a mild day and take the pup to a shallow, slow-flowing stream across which you can wade with Wellington boots. Command him to stay about three yards back from the bank and then wade across the stream. Position yourself a few yards back from the bank and then, after a few seconds pause, call him to you. When he reaches you, give petting and praise. In the event of the puppy refusing to enter the water, cross back to him, again command him to stay, re-cross to the opposite bank and coax him to you with an edible reward.

Once the dog will cross a shallow stream confidently, give him some simple dummy retrieves across a small river, gradually moving to wider and deeper sections. When he has had to actually swim part of the way with a dummy in his mouth you can assume that water will present no further problems. It only remains to practice a few retrieves with the dummy thrown into the water rather than across it. For this exercise use a pond or lake with a gently sloping bottom or a slow river so that the dummy will not be carried away by the current.

JUMPING GATES AND FENCES

Modern fences with barbed wire are an abomination but, regrettably, they exist on almost every shoot. For training purposes use gates, wooden fences or plain wire fences. If you do have to cross barbed wire, help the dog by placing your coat or game bag over the fence. Left to his own devices, a dog will naturally seek the easiest way through or round an obstruction in his path. For initial training, therefore, it is wise to arrange matters so that the only way is "over". A gate in a passageway or an enclosed pen is ideal.

Firstly, give the pup confidence in his ability to jump by commanding him to stay on one side, crossing yourself and then calling him to you. Select a fairly low obstacle for this and give him plenty of praise when he jumps it. Using the same low fence or gate, throw a dummy over it and command him to retrieve. Once he is accustomed to jumping the gate to retrieve the dummy, substitute the command "Get-over" for the normal retrieve command. After a week of jumping fences for a dummy, use the command to send him over when no dummy has been thrown.

CONSOLIDATION

At this stage in the training of your gundog it is worth spending a few weeks consolidating all of the previous exercises from the Lessons by running through a mixture of them during each training session. You should then have a confident, obedient and capable gundog to introduce to the field.

Often an older dog can be used to introduce a puppy to water

Lesson 12

Finishing School and Higher Education

Normal Age Range: 10-16 month
Normal Duration: 6-10 weeks

FUR AND FEATHER

Make the transition from dummies to cold game gradually. Start with a rabbit which has been dead for two or three days and use it as a dummy in the standard retrieving exercises, both marked and unseen. Pay particular attention to delivery to ensure that the pup gives up the rabbit as readily as he does a dummy. Birds are slightly more difficult as some dogs have an initial dislike of loose feathers. Especially if woodpigeon are used, it pays to start with the bird wrapped in a piece of muslin or a ladies' stocking.

After a week of exercises involving cold game, progress to similar work using rabbits and birds which have been freshly shot. (Do not take the dog with you when you go to shoot them.)

This is also the time to ensure that your dog is steady to live birds and animals. Take every opportunity to walk him at heel through ground which is known to contain game. Every time a bird or rabbit flushes be ready to give a blast on the stop whistle if he shows the slightest tendency to chase. If by any chance the stop whistle is disobeyed, this is one occasion when punishment is really necessary. Catch him by the scruff of the neck and, shaking and scolding simultaneously, drag him back to the exact spot where he was when the whistle was blown and command him to stay. Keep him at that point for several minutes before moving on. Also arrange access to a farmyard and walk the dog through it to subject him to the temptations of chickens and sheep. If you are in any doubt, use a check cord initially and stop the dog at the first sign of wanting to give chase.

INTO THE FIELD

The first few times you take your young dog to a shoot, do not carry a gun yourself. Concentrate on working him and let others do the shooting. When you do take him out with your own gun, it pays to only shoot at about half the game which he flushes and only send him to retrieve half of what is shot. This will help to avoid the dog assuming that everything is "his" and anticipating commands.

Throughout his working life discipline must be maintained and there are a number of simple strategies which will aid this. For example, after opening his kennel door, always command him to stay and walk 10 or 20 yards away before calling him to you. Perhaps most important of all, when a successful shot has been taken, do not send him to retrieve immediately. Unless the bird is in danger of being swept away by fast-flowing water, wait 10 or 20 seconds after the sound of the shot before sending him to pick up. Otherwise the dog will quickly come to regard the sound of gunfire to mean that he should set out on a retrieve and a dog which runs-in to shot is a menace in any shooting situation. Bad gundogs are invariably the result of a handler who has failed to maintain steadiness during the years after initial training has been completed and the statement "But I only use him for roughshooting" is rarely more than a feeble excuse for shortcomings on the handler's part.

Gundog Training FAQ

The most frequently asked questions in gundog training and care

The Gundog and Bird Dog Discussion Forum

Eric Begbie's Gundog and Bird Dog Discussion Forum was launched on the internet in 2001 and in the first four years of its existence it attracted over a million visits. Many of the visitors were novice gundog owners from all five continents who looked to the Forum for advice and guidance in the training of their gundogs. Some of the visitors were highly experienced trainers who were only too happy to offer their assistance when problems were posted and answers sought. A particularly valuable aspect of the Forum has been the international nature of the discussions. Frequently trainers in the United Kingdom will offer different advice from those in, say, the USA and this diversity allows the best of both traditions to be assessed and benefited from.

The Gundog Discussion Forum is to be found on the Internet at:

www.less-stress.com/discuss2/

Many of the regular visitors to the Forum are gundog owners who are training their dogs with the Gundog Training Broadsheets that form the basis of the first section of this book. The Broadsheets are systematically graded to match the age and stage of the gundog puppy and present a particularly clear and easy-to-follow training course for the amateur gundog trainer.

Inevitably anyone training a gundog for the first time will hit problems. This occurs because every trainer and every dog is an individual and, as in all other walks of life, individuals steadfastly refuse to conform to "averages" or "norms". Fortunately most of the problems are easily solved so long as they are tackled patiently, sensibly and with great care. Above all else, in solving training problems, it is essential to rigorously apply the three basic principles outlined in the Lessons in this book – consistency, non-predictability and insistence.

This section presents the 24 most frequently asked questions about gundog training and gundog care to arise in the first four years of the Discussion Forum. It is hoped that, when used in conjunction with the Gundog Training Broadsheets, it will be an invaluable aid to the owner and trainer of a gundog puppy.

FAQ 1 – *I have heard that gundogs should be trained to "drop to shot". Is this correct and how do I train my labrador to do it?*

Dropping to shot simply means that the dog stops and sits whenever it hears a shot being fired. It is more common for spaniel and bird dog owners to train their dogs to do this than retriever owners. With any breed it can be an effective preventive measure to avoid the opposite behaviour – running-in to shot. You really need to decide whether it is something you want your dog to do.

With a spaniel or bird dog that is hunting in front of the Gun, the sound of a shot being fired can be a useful signal to make the dog sit and watch to mark the fall. With a retriever, like a labrador, it is more usual to expect the dog to continue in a retrieve, rather than stop, if a shot is fired while it is in the process of retrieving a bird. However, the choice is yours.

To train a dog to drop to shot you simply repeat the Stop Whistle training exercise in Lesson 6, but substitute the sound of a gunshot for the whistle in the first phase when the dog is beside you and then use the sound of a shot and the whistle almost simultaneously in the second phase when the dog is at a distance. It can be very helpful to have the assistance of a friend when doing this – while the dog is romping freely, you blow the stop whistle and, immediately, your friend fires the gun.

One word of warning – do not attempt to train your dog to drop to shot before you have satisfactorily completed the exercise in Broadsheet 7 to accustom the puppy to the sound of gunshot. Also, don't train your dog to drop to shot if you ever intend entering him in retriever field trials. In trials the dog must complete a retrieve even if a shot is fired.

FAQ 2 – *Most of my shooting is wildfowling and roughshooting and I am tempted to get a multi-purpose gundog rather than a specialist breed. What would you advise?*

My first suggestion is that you should get a breed of dog that you like. For wildfowling and roughshooting virtually any breed will do although a retriever, such as a labrador, is probably best if you do a lot of shooting where many of the birds will fall in water. Spaniels can swim very well but they are less suited to long retrieves in icy water on the mid-winter foreshore.

If most of your sport is walking-up hedges and bramble thickets, then a spaniel will face denser cover than most retrievers.

By "multi-purpose gundog", I assume that you mean one of the HPR breeds such as the German shorthaired pointer. Once again it is a matter of personal preference but do be aware that most HPRs (which, incidentally, stands for Hunt, Point, Retrieve) are less suited to long swims in icy brine than a labrador and less likely to hunt through thick thorns than a spaniel. Those breeds do have a very enthusiastic following but be aware of their limitations. If most of your sport is walking-up grouse on moors or pheasants and partridges on open farmland, then an HPR could be very suitable choice. Probably the least suitable breeds for the wildfowler and roughshooter are the pure bird dog breeds such as English pointer or Gordon Setter.

FAQ 3 – *Most of the books I have read say that, when walking to heel, a dog should be trained to walk on the handler's left side. I am left handed – should I reverse this?*

The reason that dogs are normally trained to walk on the handler's left is that a right-handed person is likely to carry their gun over their right arm. It is just a little bit safer to have the dog on the other side. So, if you carry your gun over your left arm, then it would make sense to train your dog to walk at your right heel.

Having said that, some advanced handlers train their dogs to walk at either side (as indicated by the handler, not whichever the dog fancies!!!) so that they can vary the side according to circumstances, e.g. when walking along a public road. The most usual way of indicating which side the dog should adopt is a snapping of the fingers on the desired side.

Another complication arises when the handler has two dogs. Some prefer both dogs to walk on the same side; others prefer one dog to walk on either side. To a large extent it is a matter of personal choice but always have an eye on the matter of gun safety.

FAQ 4 – *The Lessons recommend using a treat such as a biscuit as a reward during very early training. At what stage should this be phased out?*

I only recommend using edible rewards during the very first "Here – Sit – Stay" training exercises with a young puppy.

The important point is to always associate the giving of a biscuit with other forms of rewards, such as verbal praise in a kindly voice and gentle petting. The purpose is to ensure that those non-edible rewards quickly become effective on their own. Remember that the purpose of rewards is to reinforce desired behavioural responses. In general terms, you should be able to stop giving edible treats within the second week of the exercises in Lesson 5. By the way, what we call biscuits in the UK are more often known as cookies in America.

FAQ 5 – *My young spaniel tends to work too far out in front and just ignores the turn signal. Help?*

It is important to start a spaniel questing at short ranges (say 10 yards) and to gradually increase its range to the maximum you desire (say 15 yards) gradually. If the dog ignores your turn whistle and hand signals during this training period, then for a while substitute the Stop Whistle for the turn signal. In other words, when the dog reaches the limit of the desired range, stop him and then give a hand signal to send him in the desired direction. If he ignores the Stop Whistle, go right back to Lesson 6 and concentrate on this before attempting to return to the questing training.

There is a balance to be struck between a wild spaniel that runs out of control and a "sticky" dog that will not hunt properly. That balance, however, must include 100% obedience to the handler's commands. Don't be misled by "gurus" who say that some level of disobedience can be allowed in a questing dog.

FAQ 6 – *My dog goes out and picks the dummy but she does not bring it right back to me. Usually she drops it about a yard in front of me. How can I cure this fault?*

This question, or varieties of it, is the most common enquiry on the Internet Forum. Variations include slow retrieves or failure to deliver to hand. In all of those cases it is necessary to "smarten up" the retrieve so that the dog picks up the dummy, comes back quickly and delivers it to the owner's hand.

If your dog is from proven working stock it will have a genetic predisposition to "fetching". It just does not know exactly what to do with the dummy once it has picked it up. Proceed as follows:

Throw a fairly short dummy. Keep the dog sitting beside you for about 10 seconds before sending him to retrieve. As soon as the dog picks the dummy up, start walking backwards away from the dog with your hand held at dummy level and calling the dog to you. In most cases this simple exercise will cause the dog to come right to you. Be prepared to receive the dummy in your hand as soon as the dog brings it to you. If this exercise does not work first time, try speeding up the rate at which you walk backwards. Remember to give the dog heaps of praise and petting when he first gets it right.

If there are problems with the puppy wanting to wander off with the dummy, instead of bringing it back towards the handler, it can help to perform this exercise in an enclosed space. A "lane" between a house wall and garden fence can be good or, if necessary, build a temporary "retrieving lane" from chicken wire. Make it about four feet wide and 25 yards long.

FAQ 7 – *My dog is reluctant to jump fences on command. What can I do to solve this problem?*

First of all, remember that you should never, never ask a dog to jump a fence with a barbed wire top strand without first placing a protector over the wire.

If the dog simply refuses to jump a normal fence on command, build a "jumping pen" with chicken wire (use the same wire as in the above FAQ) about 10 yards square. Use 3-feet netting but, to start with, bend one of the walls down so that this side is only 2 feet high. Lift the puppy into the pen, stepping in yourself. Pet the pup to get it comfortable about being inside the pen. Then step out of the pen and call the dog to you over the lower wall. If he does not come, go back into the pen, make the low wall even lower and try again. Once you have a height that the pup will jump, gradually over a period of days, increase the height of the wall. Once he will jump a three foot wall, vary the exercises by giving him retrieves, both with him starting in the pen and the dummy thrown outside and with him outside and the dummy thrown in. Once the dog is happy about jumping in and out of the pen to retrieve, start introducing the verbal "get over" command.

Most dogs love jumping fences once they have discovered that it's possible. The advantage of chicken wire is that the dog can see through it. Dogs tend to be more unsure about solid fences until they have confidence in their handler's commands.

FAQ 8 – *My gundog retrieves a dummy without any problems at all. However when I took him shooting last week he refused to pick up dead pheasants. Is there a cure for this?*

First of all you should have made a gradual transition from dummies to shot game. Some dogs have no problems at all about making the transition, some are OK with pheasants and partridges but have an aversion to a particular species, commonly woodcock or woodpigeon, and others, such as yours, are not sure about any bird to begin with. The problems may arise because the dog does not like the sensation of feathers in his mouth or because the scent of freshly shot game is unfamiliar.

Go back to your basic retrieving exercises but substitute a cold dead bird wrapped in muslin (or the foot/leg from a pair of woman's tights) for the usual dummy. Once the dog is happy retrieving the wrapped bird, use a cold but unwrapped bird. Next step is a freshly shot bird that you throw for the dog (as opposed to one that has just fallen to a gun). If you take this gradual progression from dummy to warm game over a period of three or four weeks, your dog should have no further problems. Incidentally, if the problem only exists with a particular species of bird, use the same exercise with that species wrapped in muslin.

Remember – just as with every new exercise – to give heaps of praise and petting when the dog first performs correctly.

FAQ 9 – *I have just learned that the sire of my new ESS puppy was gun shy. Is this condition hereditary and is there any cure?*

Opinion varies about whether gun shyness can be inherited but one of the reasons for always buying a puppy from good FTCh parentage is to reduce the chance of any unfortunate traits or conditions being inherited. What is certain, however, is that any puppy can be made gun-shy if its introduction to gunfire is not handled carefully.

For most pups the method in Lesson 7 will be OK but if you have any doubts about the puppy – either because a parent was allegedly gun shy or because you have noticed the pup being startled by loud noises – take it much more carefully and gradually.

Lesson 7 suggests beginning with the puppy 100 yards away from the source of the bang. With potentially sensitive pups, increase the initial distance to 250 yards and spread the gradual reduction of this distance over a longer period of time – say 4 weeks – before risking a shot at close quarters.

Remember always to accompany the sound of the shot with loads of praise and petting so that the dog grows to associate the bang with pleasurable experiences.

If you have decided to train your dog to drop to shot (see FAQ 1), then you can do this at the same time as you are accustoming the dog to the sound of gunshot.

One word of warning – it is far more difficult to cure gun shyness than to prevent it developing in the first place. So do take care when you first introduce any pup to gunfire.

FAQ 10 – *I have seen electronic training collars advertised. Are they a good idea for training a gundog?*

This topic has spawned more "Transatlantic" differences on the Gundog Discussion Forum than any other. Basically, electronic training collars are far more common and acceptable in the USA than they are in Britain.

The British thinking on this is absolutely straightforward. Over generations of careful breeding, the UK gene pools of the common gundog breeds have developed to contain a high degree of genetic predisposition to "trainability" and a natural ability to retrieve and to hunt. A puppy from good FTCh stock should be easily trained without any need for an electronic collar. The worry is that if a "hard-to-train" dog, lacking in those genetic qualities, was nevertheless successfully trained as a result of using "hard" methods, it might go on to win field trials and be subsequently bred from. This would result in a contamination of the gene pool and a dilution of the positive qualities that have been built up over generations of careful selection and breeding.

In America it is accepted that methods such as the electronic collar might be necessary in order to successfully train a dog in the shortest possible time, especially for advanced Field Trial or Hunt Test work.

My own worry is that sometimes an e-collar may be used to compensate for shortcomings in the trainer. If you feel you must use a collar, then in the UK at least, please do not breed from your dog, no matter how good a gundog it may become.

One word of caution – if you train a dog using a collar, you may have to fit it with a dummy collar whenever it is working. Dogs that have been trained with a collar are often obedient while they are wearing one but become less disciplined when the collar is removed. Again be aware of a difference between USA and UK. In Britain you will almost never see a gundog wearing any type of collar. In America it is quite common for plain fabric or leather collars to be worn, often with a rabies tag attached.

FAQ 11 – *I am intending to run my labrador in Field Trials and have been told that "normal" work such as picking-up or beating at big shoots will ruin him for this. Is this true?*

Absolute rubbish!! A friend whose labrador won the 2001 International Retriever Championship is a practising gamekeeper who takes all his dogs beating and picking-up on neighbouring shoots and they also accompany him on his rounds on his own shoot.

The more "practice" a dog gets, the better its natural abilities will develop. The only caveat is that, whenever you are working your dog, he must always be 100% under your control. In the bustle and excitement of a big shoot it may be easier to have lapses of concentration in this regard. Just be careful and concentrate on your dog rather than on what others are doing.

FAQ 12 – *My cocker spaniel behaves fine when he is on the lead. He will walk to heel without pulling and sit when told. But as soon as I let him off the* *lead he races around and ignores my shouts and whistles. I am beginning to despair. What can I do?*

This complaint – or varieties of it – is common from handlers who have neglected to concentrate sufficiently on the early obedience training. The only remedy is to go right back to the beginning and start from scratch. Take each lesson slowly, patiently and carefully and do not move on until a lesson is mastered and is performed correctly every time. 100% obedience is an essential element of gundog training.

In the meantime, do not allow the dog to run free, other than in a restricted space such as a totally enclosed small garden.

As you go back over the early lessons pay particular attention to the Stop Whistle. You must be able to stop the dog instantly at any distance before you can hope to have success with more advanced training.

Often when inadequate attention to detail in the early stages leads to indiscipline of the type mentioned in the question, the handler becomes discouraged and frustrated and this adversely affects his levels of patience. If this stage is reached during a training session it is far better to stop for the day and start afresh after both dog and trainer are rested.

One additional lesson is the "two-lead trick" that can help cure a propensity to run off as soon as the lead is removed. First of all place a longish check cord on the dog (about five yards length should be enough) and then put on an ordinary walking lead. Walk the dog on the ordinary lead for a few minutes. Then stop and remove the walking lead, taking care to have a secure grip of the check cord. If the dog runs off, give a blast on the Stop Whistle just as the puppy reaches the limit of the cord and gets stopped by it.

FAQ 13 – *When I throw a dummy for my pup he keeps looking at me rather than watching the flight of the dummy and marking the fall. How can I get him to mark where the dummy lands?*

The best solution to this problem is to do some retrieving exercises with the help of a friend. Command the pup to sit at your feet. Your friend should them make a noise to attract the pup's attention (not too loud if you have not yet reached the gunshot stage) and immediately throw the dummy. Keep the dog sitting for another few seconds before sending him to retrieve. Repeat this exercise with the dummy-throwing friend at different distances and at different positions so that the pup gets used to having to look around to see the flight of the dummy.

It can also be useful to repeat those exercises in the dark so that the pup learns to mark a fall by sound as well as by sight.

Once the dog is sufficiently steady, reinforce the marking exercise by commanding the dog to sit and stay, then walk about 20 yards away and throw a dummy from there. Then walk back to the dog before sending him to retrieve. During each training session mix all those exercises up and the dog will soon learn to mark the dummy.

FAQ 14 – *My new labrador puppy seems to be scared of water. She absolutely hates it when I try to give her a bath. As I am a keen duck hunter a dog that hates water is of no use to me. Should I give up now and get another puppy?*

You should give up trying to bath her now! Why do you do this? If a dog has an initial aversion to water trying to give it a bath is the worst thing to do. I doubt if any of my gundogs had more than three or four baths each in their lifetimes – they only got that treatment if they were really muddy. One of them never liked a bath but loved swimming and retrieving from water. I had another one that would walk around a rain puddle but swim half a mile to retrieve a goose from a stormy midwinter sea.

Most dogs will take to water like the proverbial duck so long as the first experiences of it are fun. A desperate owner trying to bathe a reluctant puppy does not sound like a fun situation.

Forget the bathing and give your pup plenty of opportunities to enter water without stress by walking him along the shore of a lake and letting him play near shallow water. Under no circumstances force him into the water at that stage.

If, by the time he is 6 – 8 months old, he has not entered water of his own accord, bring forward the simpler exercises from Lesson 11, such as coaxing the dog over a shallow and narrow stream. This is one situation where the use of an edible reward might be appropriate. It sounds a bit of a bore but, if the first attempt fails, keep looking for shallower and narrower streams until you eventually have success. Then heap praises on the puppy.

If you are already at the stage of giving retrieving training, you can also start giving some simple dummy retrieves that involve crossing a narrow shallow stream. Do "dry" retrieves across water before you move on the "wet" retrieves where the dummy is thrown into water.

FAQ 15 – *My first attempt at gundog training has gone well so far but I would like to make the dog slightly more responsive to recall and stop signals. Are there any simple exercises to achieve this?*

In a word – Yes! Once the dog performs all of the basic exercises reliably and satisfactorily you can help avoid boredom for both you and the dog by making up more complex tasks. For example, when you send a dog out to retrieve a dummy, occasionally use the Stop Whistle to stop him halfway to the dummy. On some occasions keep him on the drop for a few seconds before sending him to complete the retrieve; on other occasions call him back to you instead of completing the retrieve. Mix both those variations up with normal retrieves during each session.

The point about exercises like those is that they help avoid the undesirable situation where a dog can anticipate your commands. By having plenty of variety in a training session you avoid predictability and this is one of the main ways of keeping a gundog "sharp". He has to wait for your command rather than "guessing" what you will want him to do.

At this stage in a gundog's training it is important to give verbal praise in a kindly voice to reward correct responses. When a dog regularly gets pleasure from a kindly voice, it will only need a harsh word to "punish" any unwanted behaviour.

FAQ 16 – *When my dog gets excited it whines. I have been told that I will be sent home from shoots if I take a whining dog. What is the best way to stop this?*

Certainly no-one wants a dog that whines or barks when it is working but, once those undesirable behaviours establish themselves they can be very difficult to eradicate.

I have a friend in America who has a kennel of setters at his home. Both he and his wife are out all day and neighbours complained that the dogs sometimes barked if a vehicle passed or children were playing in the street. He solved that problem by having a sprinkler system set up in the kennel which was triggered by an acoustic release. Every time the dogs barked, they got a shower. Apparently within a few days, the unwanted barking was cured completely.

Really the only way to stop whining or barking is to punish it as soon as it starts. At the first whimper of a whine, reach down and grasp the puppy by the loose skin under his neck. Give a gentle shake and say "No!" in a loud sharp voice. A water pistol is another well-tried method and it may even be one situation where the use of an electric collar might be justified (see FAQ 10) in really bad cases. It sounds harsh but whining is a problem that must be nipped in the bud. The longer you leave it, the worse it will get.

FAQ 17 – *Should I keep my labrador puppy indoors or in an outside kennel?*

Some people have no choice and must keep their gundogs in the house and many still perform perfectly adequately. However, if you can, it is better to have a permanent kennel and run for the dog to live in. A dog that lives in a kennel and only gets out for exercise and training will regard every outing as a real pleasure and will often seem keener to please its handler. A dog kept outside is also likely to become hardier than a pooch that is kept in a centrally heated apartment.

FAQ 18 – *Should I have my dogs castrated and my bitches spayed? I have no intention of breeding from any of them and have been told they will be better behaved if they are neutered.*

I am not in favour of neutering dogs or bitches unless there are positive reasons for doing so – e.g. to reduce excessive aggressiveness in a dog or to avoid unwanted pregnancies in situations where a bitch in season simply cannot be kept apart from male dogs. If you do have a dog neutered, watch out for any inclination to become overweight.

Routine neutering seems to be more acceptable in America than in Britain but I have seen no evidence to suggest that it makes a dog or bitch more trainable or better behaved. I sometimes think that some dogs and bitches are subjected to unnecessary surgery, more for the convenience of the owners than for the welfare of the dogs.

FAQ 19 – *I read that dogs that are bred and trained for Field Trials are too highly strung to be of any use as ordinary hunting and retrieving dogs. Yet in the Lessons you recommend getting a puppy from "proven working stock". What is the difference?*

None. The people who say that there is a difference between Field Trial dogs and ordinary working dogs simply haven't a clue what they are talking about. The qualities that make a good Field Trial dog are exactly the same qualities that the ordinary shooting man or woman needs to have in his or her dog. That applies irrespective of whether they participate in waterfowling or upland game hunting.

There are, of course, no guarantees in genetics but you certainly increase the chance of getting a good, easily trainable dog with the natural instincts for retrieving, hunting, etc. if you buy a puppy from well established Field Trial lines. My preference would be for a puppy whose sire and dam are both Field Trial Champions (FTCh) but, if such a puppy is not available, go for one whose sire is a FTCh and whose dam is a proven working bitch with at least one of its parents a FTCh.

FAQ 20 – *Can you tell me the difference between Field Trials and Working Tests and what about the sort of events that are held at Game and Country Fairs? Can anyone enter them?*

In Britain Field Trials are staged to emulate as closely as possible a normal shooting day. The line of Guns walks-up game in the usual way with the dogs and their handlers in the line. Like a normal shoot, there is unpredictability about what will flush, where it will go and whether it will be shot. When a bird or rabbit is shot, the judges decide which dog should be sent to retrieve. Although judges will try to give each dog a fair selection of work to do, it is in the nature of Trials that there is a lot of luck involved.

In America, Field Trials are more "artificial" as there is a degree of standardisation in the exercises and sometimes reared birds are released in ways that would be illegal in Britain. Although they may be artificial, American Trials probably do give each dog a fairer chance as some, but not all, of the luck element will be eliminated.

Working tests use dummies instead of live game. Each dog can, therefore, be given the same selection of marked retrieves, blind retrieves, double or treble retrieves, etc.

Game Fairs and Country Fairs often have informal working tests and also, very often, a "scurry" where each dog simply does one or two retrieves against the clock and the fastest one wins. Anyone can enter scurries but working tests usually have to be entered in advance.

If you want to enter Field Trials in the UK, your dog must be KC registered and you should join one or more of your local gundog clubs. Entries for Field Trials are often heavily oversubscribed and you may have to submit entries for several before you get accepted for one.

Whatever route you take – good luck.

FAQ 21 – *My GSP bitch has turned out really well and I would like to have pups from her but I am worried that, at 6 years of age, she may be too old to have a litter. Is there any danger in breeding from a bitch of this age?*

The first thing to say is that before considering breeding from any bitch, irrespective of age, have her checked out by your vet. He will advise you on the feeding, worming and supplements the bitch will need both before mating and during pregnancy.

On the question of age, the usual advice is not to take a first litter from a bitch before the age of 2 or after the age of 5. However, a fit and active 6 year old may be OK – check with your vet first though, just to be sure.

A bitch that has had a litter can have subsequent litters for a few years beyond the 5 year old stage.

Just a word of caution – don't take a litter from a bitch just because you want a puppy for yourself. Make sure that you will be able to find homes for all the other pups before you decide to take this step. Another consideration is that there seems to be some evidence that having a single litter can increase the chance of some illnesses in later life. Vets often recommend that a bitch that has had a litter should have at least one more within a three year period to reduce such risks. Discuss this with your own vet and take his advice.

FAQ 22 – *I am considering getting an English Springer Spaniel puppy to train for roughshooting. Should I get one with a docked tail and should the dew claws have been removed?*

On the first question I am 100% certain that any roughshooting ESS or cocker should have its tail docked. The chance of serious damage to an undocked tail when a spaniel is hunting through thickets of brambles and thorns is too high to take the risk. There are some other breeds that were traditionally docked for purely cosmetic reasons and I am not in favour of mutilating dogs for "vanity" purposes.

In Britain there are fewer and fewer vets willing to dock dogs' tails as the official RCVS advice is against it. However there is a Council of Docked Breeds that campaigns on behalf of working spaniel owners (amongst others) and they maintain a list of vets throughout the country who will undertake this task. You can contact the Council of Docked Breeds on www.cdb.com and there are similar organisations in Australia and New Zealand. Note that it is now illegal in Britain for an unqualified person to dock a dog's tail.

Dew claws are a more controversial subject. Personally I have never had dew claws removed from any of my dogs and I have never had any that experienced problems as a result. However other people claim that damage can occur if the dew claws are not removed, especially if the dog is going to be working thick cover. I suggest that you consult your own vet about this and explain to him the type of work your spaniel will be doing.

FAQ 23 – *My labrador's tail bleeds at the tip whenever I take her beating on a local shoot. What can I do to avoid this?*

If your dog's tail heals between occurrences of this problem, then you can guard against it by simply covering the tip of the tail (the last four inches should be enough) with muslin and securing it with insulating tape before you take her out beating.

On the other hand, if the tip of the tail never properly heals, then there will be a risk of infection and you need to consult a vet. One of my labradors had this problem and her tail would even bleed as a result of wagging it against the kennel walls when she sensed feeding time was approaching. Eventually the vet had to shorten her tail by a couple of inches. Once the "amputation" had healed, she never had any trouble with a bleeding tail again.

This is actually a very common complaint with labs as the coat at the tip of their tails can be quite thin. Other retriever breeds, such as goldies or flatcoats tend to have thicker hair on their tails. Incidentally a vet friend of mine says that the most common cause of injury to dogs' tails is having them caught in a car door. Always be careful that the tail is right inside before slamming a door!

FAQ 24 – *I have a labrador and a springer. I feed them both with a well known all-in-one dried food and give quantities according to the instructions on the sack. My lab is very overweight and the spaniel is also a bit heavy round the middle. What should I do?*

The quantity instructions on any food pack can only be approximate as different dogs of the same breed and weight can have quite different metabolism patterns and different levels of activity. A dog that is working hard during the winter will need more food then than it does outwith the hunting season in the summer.

Dogs like labradors and springer spaniels should have a clearly discernible "waist" and you should be ably to see the outlines of their ribs unless they have very thick coats.

Rather than take drastic action, cut back the amount of food you give them gradually over a period of a month and see how their weights respond. Don't drop down below two-thirds of the recommended quantities without firstly consulting your vet.

The other, obvious, thing is to ensure that you are giving the dogs plenty of vigorous exercise to keep them fit for next season. A gundog that works hard during the shooting season should be given a lot more than just a couple of half-mile walks each day during the close season.

Supplementary Guidance

This section has been provided to give supplementary information to gundog owners who are training their dogs using the Lessons in this book. It will be of particular interest to readers in North America where training methods are occasionally different from those practiced in Britain and Europe.

Topic 1 - Training Methods

The Lessons in this training course were designed to present dog owners with a training method that does not involve any level of cruelty. Gundogs from good working lines, irrespective of whether they are labradors, springer spaniels or HPRs, should have the natural abilities and instincts to enable them to be trained to the very highest standards without resorting to "pressure" training methods that involve subjecting a puppy to pain or discomfort. For amateur gundog work, techniques such as the use of electric shock collars, smacking or pinching ears should be unnecessary if the dog has the required natural abilities and the trainer has the requisite degree of patience and respect for his dog.

This is why it is essential that a puppy intended for use as a gundog or bird dog must be chosen from Field Trial stock. In Britain such dogs should have a genetic predisposition to easy training by humane methods and possess natural hunting and retrieving instincts. Even if the dog is only intended for use in roughshooting (upland game hunting) or wildfowling (waterfowling), it really pays to start with a puppy from Field Trial parentage.

In America it is recommended that you try to obtain a puppy from a litter where both parents were demonstrably trained to a high standard by humane methods. (Sometimes in USA trainers who are successful in this respect are colloquially known as "Amish Trainers".)

Topic 2 - Early Days

The graduated Lessons in this book suggest that a formal approach to basic obedience training should begin at the age of 3 or 4 months. As it is common

50

to obtain a puppy at the age of about 7 weeks, some owners have asked how the first few weeks of their puppy ownership should be spent.

The short answer is that this very early stage in a puppy's life should be spent having fun, playing games, getting used to its new home and owner and generally becoming conditioned to a few basic rules.

There will be lots of occasions every day, especially if the puppy is being kept in your house, rather than in an outside kennel, when the puppy will do things that can either be encouraged or discouraged. In fact, this is an ideal time to establish tone of voice as tool that you will use frequently in future training. Tone of voice is one of the most powerful reinforcement and punishment agents you will have in a humane training regime.

To begin with, use a kind "Good Boy (or Girl)", along with a small edible treat and some physical petting to reward any action that you want to encourage. Conversely, use "Bad Dog!", "Down" or a simple "No!" in a harsh tone of voice, along with gentle physical correction, as a punishment or deterrent to stop an action that you want to discourage. For example if you call the puppy's name and he comes to you (purely from inquisitiveness at this stage as you have not yet trained him), praise him in a kind voice and reward with petting and/or a treat. If he makes as if to chew an electric lamp cable, tell him "No!" in a harsh voice and gently lift him away from the cable by the scruff of the neck. Similarly, if you are sitting in a chair and he rears up to place his front paws on your knees, command "Down!" in a harsh voice and gently lift him down to the floor. Remember that he will also be conditioned by the words you use - so use them consistently and avoid words that you may want to use as other commands later in training.

Think critically about everything you and your puppy do at this stage in his life - you will be surprised by just how many opportunities there are to establish early training. The important factor is to be clear and consistent in the messages you give.

The other important aspect of these early days is in the games you play with your puppy. Watch any litter of young puppies and you will notice that they play lots of boisterous games with each other, followed by frequent spells of sleep. When you bring home your puppy, you are taking it away from its litter mates and the puppy will want to play the same games with you. There are two golden rules that apply to this period of play:

(a) Do not allow games that involve behaviour that will be regarded as undesirable later on. The prime example is "tug o' war" where the puppy takes something into his mouth and invites you (or so it seems) to try to pull it away from him. Avoid this game at all costs.

(b) Clearly establish a difference between objects (such as toys and chews) that are OK for the puppy to play with, and objects (such as your shoe laces or purse) that are "yours" and not OK to play with. Again use tone of voice to indicate the difference. This is an important differentiation as, once you start retriever training, it is important that the puppy does not regard the training dummy as "his" toy.

Finally, as you get to know your puppy and become confident with him, there is no harm in bringing some of the simplest formal obedience exercises forward a week or two. In play or in everyday routines, there may be opportunities to introduce "Sit" and "Here" a little earlier than the Lessons suggest. But do not be over-eager; patience is a real virtue, especially in the early days of dog training.

Topic 3 - Use of Heavier Gundog Training Dummies

Most of the basic gundog training will be carried out using canvas dummies that weigh about 1 lb (0.45 Kg). This is an ideal weight for most purposes.

However, from about 10 months of age, it can be advantageous to introduce a heavier dummy for occasional use. Dummies weighing 2 lbs and 3 lbs are available and one of each is a useful addition to the trainer's armoury.

Apart from accustoming the dog to retrieving heavier objects in preparation for work with birds and rabbits, the heavier dummies also encourage the puppy to lift and hold an object in a well balanced way. Do be careful not to introduce heavier dummies too early as, if it is physically impossible for the puppy to lift them easily, he may resort to dragging them by the toggle.

Topic 4 – The Difference between Teaching and Training

In common with many other British gundog trainers I was brought up on the excellent foundations laid down by experts such as the late Peter Moxon. His philosophy was very well founded in psychological theory although, to be honest, he was probably working intuitively rather than from any scientific base.

Possibly the one factor that those experts failed to appreciate was that gundog work is, essentially, a two-stage process. Apart from such natural instincts that a puppy may possess, it really does not know what we expect it to do. It follows, therefore, that we must firstly *teach* the puppy what we want him to do. Only when we have taught him the required behaviour can we *train* him to perform it consistently every time we issue the appropriate command.

So, throughout your gundog training bear this in mind: First you must teach the dog to perform a given action in response to a given command. Then you must train him to perform that response to the command first time, every time.

Topic 5 – Have Fun – and RELAX!

When both the handler and the dog are enjoying their training routines, everything goes well. When the dog is bored or the handler is frustrated, it all falls apart.

That is probably the greatest truism contained in this book and everyone who has successfully trained a gundog will recognise the truth in the statement.

So, to maximize the return on your training effort, keep it fun. Stop any training session when it ceases to be enjoyable for either you or your puppy and make a point of ending every training session with an exercise that you know the dog will perform successfully, in order that you can finish with some praise and petting.

Choice of Puppy

Dogs come in all shapes and sizes and many folk are astounded to learn that all breeds of the domestic dog, from a poodle to a Great Dane, are varieties of the same species of animal. Over the centuries and in different parts of the world, many of those breeds have been used for hunting and retrieving but the choice facing the waterfowler is probably restricted to the labrador, flatcoated retriever, golden retriever or one of the springer spaniels. It is not unknown for wildfowlers to venture below the sea wall with a German shorthaired pointer or another of the HPR breeds but such sportsmen probably engage in other branches of shooting and chose their canine companion to suit a varied schedule of work on the moor or in the coverts. Indeed, the upland game hunter might well be drawn to one of those varieties.

It would be easy to sit on the fence and simply state that the shooting enthusiast would be well served by any of the proven varieties of gundog but, in reality, the newcomer to the sport will probably have greatest likelihood of success if he chooses a labrador as his first dog. All other things being equal, a good labrador from sound working stock will be more easily trained by a novice than most other breeds and it will be more forgiving of the mistakes which are certain to be made by an inexperienced trainer. The labrador is an excellent water dog, is sufficiently strong to swim a long distance carrying a goose and the breed is normally endowed with a goodly degree of patience. Having cut his teeth on a labrador, the sportsman or woman may later wish to progress to a springer spaniel, flatcoat or even an Irish water spaniel. It is all a question of personal preference and, as many, many hours will be spent alone with the beast in the countryside, it is clearly essential that the sporting gunner actually likes his or her dog!

Purchasing a puppy can be a very chancy business and the novice should take every precaution at this stage. It cannot be stressed too emphatically that no dog should be considered which is not from established working stock. There is really no need to buy a pup from the fellow around the corner when every issue of the weekly and monthly shooting periodicals carries a lengthy list of advertisements for litters which are registered with the Kennel Club and have field trial honours recorded on both sides of the pedigree. Occasionally the sporting press is engulfed by controversy regarding the suitability of field trial dogs for general shooting but there can be no doubt whatsoever that a puppy from established trial parentage is more likely to have a genetic predisposition to successful training. It is also far less likely to suffer from inborn faults such as hard-mouth or gun-shyness.

It can be reassuring to see the mother working at the time of inspecting a litter of pups and even more encouraging if the youngsters are old enough to have begun their initial schooling. A twelve week old puppy which will sit to command and come when called is likely to respond positively to further training. It is important to obtain evidence that neither parent suffers from any hereditary ailment such as hip dysplasia or retinal problems and, if the pup is more than 12 weeks old, a vaccination certificate should be obtained from the breeder.

Housing, Feeding and Health

It is tempting to keep a gundog as a family pet and some gundog owners have no alternative. There are, however, many advantages to be gained from housing the dog in an outside kennel if this is possible. Any retriever which will be required to swim in near-freezing water and wait patiently by the fowler's side in sub-zero conditions needs to be a very hardy animal and a dog which had been cosseted in a centrally heated flat is unlikely to take kindly to an early morning dip in icy brine. There can also be no argument that a gundog is more easily trained if it is quartered outside, well away from spouses, children and other confusing influences. It will come to regard every training and exercise period as a real pleasure and will be keen to please its handler.

A labrador or springer spaniel will exist very happily in a wooden kennel measuring 6ft wide by 4ft deep by 4ft high with a 6ft square run attached. Freedom from draughts and damp is crucial and the run should have a concrete base so that rainwater will drain away quickly and the dog cannot dig itself out. For the kennel itself, the most suitable material is overlapping weatherboard although well creosoted exterior ply on a softwood frame may be used as an alternative. One-third of the interior of the kennel should take the form of a raised shelf or box to provide a snug sleeping area. If straw or any other form of bedding is used in winter, it should be changed regularly to avoid skin vermin. In summer no such bedding is really necessary.

A material that I have recently discovered is "cow matting" which is available in 6-foot by 4-foot sheets from agricultural suppliers. This takes the form of a thick semi-rigid mat of high-density plastic which is soft and warm to the touch, immensely durable (it is designed to line the concrete floors of cattle barns) and can be hosed down for cleaning. It is the ideal flooring for a kennel and dispenses with any need to use auxiliary bedding. In fact, I have now covered the slabs of my external run with the same sheeting.

An adequate diet is clearly important if a gundog is to be kept in peak working condition. Cooked meat or offal mixed with biscuit meal is the traditional dinner for a dog and adopting this practice allows the protein content to be maintained while the amount of carbohydrate may be varied to meet the energy requirements of the individual dog, hence avoiding any tendency towards obesity. It is far more convenient, on the other hand, to use an all-in-one dog meal which, if purchased in 15kg or 20kg sacks, is extremely economical. There are several excellent brands of kibble specifically formulated for working dogs and most contain all of the necessary oils, vitamins and minerals.

Just one word of warning about all-in-one foods. If you are using the puppy version for gundog breeds up to a year old, be sure to select the "large breed" variety.

Canine health is rarely a serious problem for the gundog owner. Given adequate housing and a sensible diet, his gundog's mode of life will maintain it at a level of fitness which is often denied to the average household pet. Nevertheless, it is essential that the puppy is vaccinated against distemper, hardpad, jaundice and parvo-virus and that booster injections are given as prescribed by the veterinary surgeon. The outlay on such treatment is minimal when compared to the cost of curative medicine should the dog become ill.

It is also worth repeating at this point that, when selecting a puppy, ensure that both parents were certified as having low hip scores and were free from eye defects.

A Personal Tale

Hopefully, the lessons contained in this book will have shown just how straightforward the training of a gundog can be of the basic psychological principles are observed and most of the mystique is stripped away. So, finally, here is an extract from one of my earlier books, *Fowler in the Wild*, which will, I hope, provide any additional motivation that is required. I believe that this simple story perfectly illustrates the bond that can develop between a hunter and his dog. Read on.......

Old Meg was turning decidedly grey around the muzzle when Moy arrived upon the scene. The younger, slimmer bitch was entirely different in almost every respect and, from the beginning, demonstrated the potential to become and remain a top class gundog. Admittedly I took considerably greater care with her training but this was aided by a degree of overt dependence whereby her whole life, outside the kennel, was dedicated to pleasing her lord and master. Although her temperament in this respect was a huge bonus when shooting grouse or pheasant, it had a number of disadvantages below the sea wall. For example, while patiently awaiting morning flight, she spent her time watching me rather than scanning the sky for approaching duck. Only when a shot was fired would her eyes turn to mark down the falling bird and then, unlike Meg, she remained rock steady until sent to retrieve.

Despite Meg's advancing age there was a period of several years when both labradors accompanied me on fowling expeditions. If either Peter or Leon came along, bringing their own dogs, then the pack of black labs present would frequently exceed the number of duck or geese to be retrieved.

During this time we tended to favour the north shore of one of the larger estuaries and, although the trip entailed a fairly long drive, there were few Saturday mornings when Leon, with Foss occupying most of the space in the rear of his van, did not pick me up at some really unearthly hour. I very much doubt if dogs relate to each other in the same way as people do but, on those early morning forays, it always seemed that Meg and Foss were the closest of friends while Moy remained aloof, appearing to prefer human company.

Some of those mornings were spent at a spot halfway along the shore of the Firth where a public road ran down almost to the water's edge. Cars could be parked close to a small natural harbour and fowlers would walk along the top of the broad sea wall in either direction to find a hiding place in the dense belt of reeds which lined high water mark. In many respects this was "tame" wildfowling as it was very common to return from a flight without ever having stepped on to soft mud nor crawled along a flooded gutter. The attraction of that place derived not only from the ease of access but also from the fact that, a few hundred yards offshore, lay several long mudbanks which were covered by only the highest spring tides. If undisturbed, geese would roost on those banks and, when flighting off at dawn, might pass over the grassy sea wall just within shotgun range.

It is tempting, years later, to look back on those days with a measure of disdain, feeling perhaps that wilder opportunities to do business with the fowl should have been sought. They were, however, pleasant outings during which there was much to be seen. While seated comfortably against a banking, sheltered from the wind, wrens, goldcrests and a variety of tits might be watched as they flitted amongst the swaying stalks of the high reeds. In midwinter, when natural feeding was scarce, those tiny birds lost all caution and would come within a few feet of an armed wildfowler to hungrily devour a carelessly dropped sandwich crumb or other titbit. As daylight strengthened, great flocks of fieldfares swooped low over the foreshore, their "chack-chack" calls mingling with the whoosh of a thousand wings. Sometimes teal might unwittingly drop into the ditch which ran behind the sea wall and then, discovering that they had unwelcome human company, spring vertically into the air to effect their escape. Little did those diminutive duck know that, although only a few yards above high water mark, they were safe from the guns of shore-bound fowlers. Less secure were the pheasants which occasionally strayed from the adjacent estate on to the shore. Much to the chagrin of the laird's gamekeeper, as soon as his precious charges crossed the tideline, they became legitimate quarry and, on mornings when the greylag or pinkfoot skeins had passed too high or too wide, consolation might be obtained in the form of an errant longtail.

Unfortunately, but perhaps inevitably, the lure of the geese roosting on the mudbanks grew too tempting for some fowlers and it became common practice for boats to be taken out before dawn from the town on the south shore of the estuary. Then, instead of the chirping of small birds and the piping of waders, the early morning silence was rudely broken by the sound of outboard motors revving in mid-channel. Not surprisingly, the area was soon forsaken by the geese and, to the best of my knowledge, they have not returned to that part of the Firth in the numbers which Leon and I used to see.

Knowing that the great grey flocks were still in the general vicinity, we explored farther east and eventually discovered that the greylag were frequenting the wide mudflats of a large bay some seven miles along the shore. The terrain was so treacherous that, at low tide, no-one could approach within three-quarters of a mile of the roost and, in those circumstances, only a force-8 gale would cause the birds to remain within gunshot range as they flighted inland to feed. For this reason we normally timed our visits to coincide with a flowing tide in the hope that the greys would begin their daily journey from a point closer to the narrow belt of saltmarsh which skirted the shoreline. That bay was the scene of one of the few sorties when the services of Meg, Moy and Foss were required simultaneously.

Pulling in to a disused farm track, Leon switched off the engine of his rusting van and, immediately, we could hear the calling of greylag close to hand. Despite the sky still being pitch black, we feared that the geese might flight early so, without wasting any time, we donned our thigh waders and waxproofs and hurried down to the foreshore.

It was a bitterly cold January morning with the merest smattering of powdery snow clinging to each blade of grass on the hard, rutted marsh. Even where the tide had washed only a few hours earlier, the penetrating chill of midwinter had crispened the surface of the saltings so that each footstep crunched in the darkness. Drawn ever onwards by the anserine chorus, we at last found our progress blocked by the deep gully of a stream which meandered parallel to the sea wall before turning out to join the waters of the estuary. Knowing that the flock of greylag was not more than 300 yards in front, we sought cover in the reeded verges of the little river and settled down to await the coming of daylight.

Despite two layers of thick thermal stockings my feet were soon numb with the cold and my beard grew brittle as condensation froze in it at every breath. When a yellow and purple false dawn changed, quite abruptly, to the weak pinks and blues of a new morning the temperature seemed to drop a few more degrees and I began to have a serious concern that my fingers might be incapable of operating the safety catch and trigger of my gun.

Happily the geese did not tarry unduly on the shore that day. Well before sunrise they grew restless and, perhaps spurred into early flight by the sub-zero conditions, rose from the frozen mudflats in a single skein which came towards us fast and low. Because the long line of greys was little more than 20 yards high, it was possible for the shots to be taken while they were still well out in front. Presented with such an ideal opportunity, no mistakes were made and Leon and I were rewarded with one of the very rare achievements of a right-and-left each. Indeed, I cannot think of any other morning when we concurrently scored a double.

One of my birds dropped into the water of the stream while the other three fell on the far side of the gully. Without waiting to be sent, Meg lept into the river and, pushing iceflows aside with her muzzle, paddled out to collect the floating greylag. I sent Moy to pick my other goose and, as she swam across towards the opposite bank, I noticed that Foss was already preparing to re-enter the water with the first of Leon's birds in his mouth.

Its amazing how jubilation banishes discomfort. Once all four geese had been retrieved, we stood for several minutes discussing the flight and scanning the distant mud for any sign of more fowl before turning to leave the marsh. That was when we became aware that, instead of three black labradors, we were accompanied by dogs which had turned white. Millions of tiny ice crystals sparkled in their thick coats yet they did not appear to be in the least troubled by their condition. It is little wonder that labradors are so popular as wildfowling dogs - the evolution of their distant ancestors in the arduous climate of Newfoundland has fitted them perfectly to cope with the extremes of our own winters.

The next few years witnessed a marked expansion of my kennel. Moy produced an excellent litter of pups, two of which - Flight and Teal - remained with me until their training was complete and gave a great deal of pleasure before going off to work for other sportsmen. Another of that litter, Spartan Lady, was trained by Jim Munro to achieve high honours in the field trial world, including two remarkable performances in the International Gundog League Retriever Championship. Much as I enjoyed putting young dogs through their schooling, however, I never seemed to have time to become personally involved in competitive activity. My principal criterion for judging a gundog remained its prowess on the wild marsh, pheasant covert or upland moor.

In the intervening years several more gundogs have passed through my household but, when in maudlin mood, it is always to the days of Meg and Moy that my thoughts turn.

Some Websites for Gundog Trainers

Gundog Training Equipment Online Shop:

www.train-your-dogs.co.uk/shop.htm

Gundog and other Country Sports Books (UK and USA):

www.premier-pages.co.uk/books-1/

Gundog Training Magazine Online:

www.gundog-magazine.com

Gundog and Bird Dog Discussion Forums:

www.less-stress.com/discuss2/

Gundogs Galore:

www.gundogweb.co.uk

Wildfowling Information:

www.wildfowling.co.uk

Gundog Training Information:

www.train-your-dogs.co.uk

A small dummy for early training....

.....moving on to cold game later

Teach jumping using fences without any barbed wire

Printed in Great Britain
by Amazon